123 Kindergarten
Everything your child needs to learn before kindergarten

123 Kindergarten
Everything your child needs to learn before kindergarten

Barbara Allisen,
B.A., B.Ed., E.C.S., D.P.E., CCHT

With Gratitude

A child comes home from the first day at school and the parents ask,
"What did you learn at school, today?"
The child replies, "Not enough, I have to go back tomorrow!
Anonymous

To the hundreds of children, parents and caregivers
who have shared their todays and tomorrows with me.

To my own children, Kerry-Ellen and Colin;
I am a better teacher because of being your mother.

The Universe is one great Kindergarten.
Orison Swett Marden

Table of Contents

Introduction
Kindergarten Readiness

some excited and anxious children
+ some nervous and proud parents
_____

kindergarten

Any way you add it up, going to kindergarten is exciting. Another one of those firsts, along with all the rest, from first tooth, first step, first words, first time howled all night and now, First Day at School. This new first is the beginning of more than a decade at school--maybe as much as two decades, or even three!

Anticipated secondary graduations to 2099

starting school in 2010	>	**graduates 2023**
starting school in 2011	>	**graduates 2024**
starting school in 2012	>	**graduates 2025**
starting school in 2013	>	**graduates 2026**
starting school in 2014	>	**graduates 2027**
starting school in 2015	>	**graduates 2028**
starting school in 2016	>	**graduates 2029**
starting school in 2017	>	**graduates 2030**
starting school in 2086	>	**graduates 2099**

As a kindergarten teacher, it's quite understandable that I think kindergarten is a pivotal year at school. Here are just three reasons why it is so vital:

- It marks the transition between home and school.
- It is a huge expansion of the child's world.
- It has a major impact on a child's entire education.

Others think it's essential, too, and research bears this out, *internationally.*

Children who are ready for school from the day they start kindergarten have a better chance to do well in each grade and finish high school. (Human Early Learning Partnership—HELP—UBC, January 2010)

Research demonstrates that [readiness] increases a child's chances of succeeding in school and in life. Children… are less likely to be held back a grade, less likely to need special education and more likely to graduate from high school. (The PEW Charitable Trusts, 2005 Pre-K Now)

The impact of kindergarten goes beyond high school to affect our communities. One report estimated the financial cost "...*due to children entering kindergarten unprepared for school success...*" to be in the millions of dollars! (Wilder Research, The cost burden to Minnesota K-12 when children are unprepared for kindergarten, Prepared for the Bush Foundation; Chase, Coffee-Borden, Anton, Moore, Valorose, December, 2008)

All over the United States and Canada, children are entering school unprepared for the learning opportunities and challenges. Unfortunately, children who start behind often stay behind and may not even finish school. No wonder parents and caregivers are concerned with the issue of readiness. Preparing children for success in school needs to start at home, and at daycare, too. And, we all know that parents are children's first teachers. But what to teach kids and how to teach them? When are children ready to learn different concepts? Where to start? What to do if a child is struggling? What indicates possible developmental lags? Why do some things seem easier for girls and some seem easier for boys?

There are so many questions and so few places that can answer them. This book is one of those places. With over 30 years experience in preschool and kindergarten classrooms, countless inservice sessions and workshops, I have been answering parents' questions. As a parent, myself, I have walked the walk, not just talked the talk. This book outlines what to teach and:

- has tons of practical, parent-and-kid friendly how-to strategies,
- provides clues about when children are

developmentally ready, and

- can help you with where to find space for it all in super-busy days.

The activities are suitable for *all* preschool children, not just those heading off to kindergarten. Preparation for school needs to start early. Younger brothers and sisters in the family often learn the songs and the routines and enjoy the books of their older siblings in kindergarten. They wonder why they can't go to school, too. Their turn is easier because they are already familiar with many of the expectations. This book is intended to address learning concerns for the early childhood years, 0 and up.

Whether your child is off to public school in the next few years or you intend to home school, this book is also helpful. The home-schooled child will have increased demands and expectations, too, and will need to be prepared for the new learning challenges and expanded routines.

It's only natural to have questions about how best to prepare children for school and how to support them along the way. The following three questions are fundamental and cover many of the others. Throughout the book, we'll use these questions to keep us on track.

How do I know if
my child is ready
for kindergarten?

What does my child
need to learn before
kindergarten?

How do I best get my
child ready and provide
ongoing support?

Before getting into answers for these questions, I've included a developmental checklist of basic skills and developmental readiness. While these are guidelines for children closer to the age of 5, they are useful for younger children, as well. They provide the information you need as to where to go and what to do beforehand. You can use this learning and readiness checklist right now, either at home or in a care center.

Additionally, there is information as to how to rate or evaluate your child. I will apologize now for the following reminder because I will use it so often:

This is only a general guideline of basic development.

Please remember that each child is an individual and that there are differences for all children. Even though children will follow a similar pattern of development and maturation, each child has unique strengths, and weaknesses, and needs.

Quick Developmental Checklist

Children develop at their own pace
and in their own time.

Nevertheless, by the age of five, most children have developed the following skills and abilities. This is by no means a comprehensive developmental checklist; these are general indicators that can be used as a guideline tool to help you evaluate your child's readiness potential.

There is a 1-4 rating scale included below. You can use it to rate each item. Additionally, each area of the checklist will be expanded in Section B, with ideas, explanations, suggestions, and answers to many of your questions.

Self-help skills and Emotional readiness

- able to take care of bathroom needs
- washes/dries hands
- mostly independent in dressing
- able to separate from parents or caregivers for short periods of time
- recognizes, identifies and appropriately expresses basic emotions with beginning self-control

Communicative skills

- speaks understandably in 5-6 word sentences
- responds to basic requests
- follows 2-part directions
- draws pretend word scribbles or letter strings

Social skills

- enjoys playing with others of own age
- able to share a toy or game
- is comfortable in small groups of peers

Motor skills

- hops on one foot
- jumps up and lands on both feet
- walks up and down stairs, usually alternating feet
- runs at various speeds (especially if you've asked them to walk!)
- places 6-10 blocks on top of each other in a tower
- completes a simple puzzle of 7 or more pieces
- able to copy a cross figure (+) and a circle
- draws a person figure with head and 4 more body parts
- copies some letters in his/her name
- holds scissors in one hand and cuts within ½ inch on either side of a line

Pre-academic skills

- rote counts 1-10
- able to accurately count objects 1-5
- copies a simple pattern
- sorts objects into groups using color, size or shape
- able to identify same or different
- recognizes rhyming sounds
- listens to short stories without interrupting
- sings a simple song

Checklist Rating Scale

As we look at, discuss, and touch on (for visual, auditory and kinesthetic learning styles) each of these areas, here is a simple evaluation aid.

Pencil in the numbers 1,2,3, or 4 beside each point. Note an overall number, too, for each section.

1 indicates a skill that is not yet developed.
2 indicates a skill that is developing but the child is not yet all that comfortable or consistent.
3 indicates a skill that is developed for the most part and the child is quite comfortable.
4 indicates a skill that is well developed and the child is onto the next level.

Now, if your own personal learning style is visual or touch rather than verbal, think of a race:

1 being at the gate, warming up,
2 in position, you can see those skill muscles starting to work and the body focussing on the task,
3 off and running down the track and
4 reached the finish line.

You can assign these 1,2,3,and 4's yourself to your child and see at a glance a summary of readiness.

I can see, hear, and feel a question popping up, already: What if my child only gets 1's and 2's? This does NOT mean you need to panic. It indicates that your child could benefit from some extra time and attention to these issues. We will explore how to do that on the following pages.

No matter what numbers you write down, I will give you ideas you can use to help your child.

I know you have heard and read this many times before, and you will continue to hear this as your child goes through school: *children develop at different rates*. What you will likely jot down is a mixture of 1s, 2s, 3s, and 4s. Even a page covered with 4's doesn't entirely predict kindergarten readiness. You must also factor in *how* your child learns. You know your own child best. Going over this checklist is just another way to look at the question of readiness not the only way.

Please remember, this is NOT an evaluation of the *children*. Rather, it is a quick, ballpark measurement of children's *development*.

Will I be at school a long time?

Part One
Basic Readiness and Development: Skills and Remediation, Both

See Mommy... I put my stripes on myself!

Chapter One
B = By Myself

Self-help Skills

In the self-help and emotional readiness segment there are 5 points that cover basic, representative skills that a child needs at school. A child should: be able to take care of bathroom needs, wash/dry hands, be mostly independent in dressing, be able to separate from parents or caregivers, and show some level of emotional growth and control.

Can your child go to the bathroom alone and take care of wiping needs? Most need reminders to close the door, flush and wash hands--that's okay. Some kids have a not-so-subtle pee-pee dance which makes it easier for the teacher to check if somebody really needs to go for a washroom visit. However, not all children are comfortable letting the teacher know s/he needs a bathroom break. There can be other issues, too. Some don't like the door closed, or they can't figure out the handles, or they don't like so many people in the school bathroom, especially if older grades share the washroom. Set aside some time to check your child's confidence level about bathroom issues. This one is somewhat easy to evaluate and to give a 1,2,3, or 4. Most of the time, support is straightforward.

If you give your child just a 1 or 2 for bathroom skills, practice the skills needed and talk about them. A child with a 3 or 4, may need some talk-time, too. For some children, the bathroom is a quiet, private space and they may take considerable time to use the restroom. This is acceptable at home but not at school. Going over bathroom issues may be helpful for these children, too.

Father - What's that? Sounds like a hundred drums!
Mother - No, it's Junior doing the peepee dance.

Because of security and safety issues, lots of boys are used to using the women's restroom with their moms. Some of them may not have seen or used urinals. This might be something to check. And, practice what the words Boys and Girls look like, not just the picture symbols. Just in case. Schools do not use "Men" and "Ladies" on the restroom doors.

Most children need reminders to wash and dry their hands. Some will need more than reminders, they'll need checks: Are you sure you washed? And they may require prompts:

Hmm, just in case, give those hands another wash. Germs can hide. The point is *can* your child wash and dry hands independently, rather that *does*. Schools sometimes seem like germ factories, so good hand washing is important.

This is Not on the checklist, but is important for you: speaking of germs.... Kindergarten is also the first time some of the children come into contact with such a variety of colds, flus and other assorted bacteria and viruses. Staying well can be a challenge during the kindergarten year, *for the whole house!* If this is your first one going off to school, be forewarned. Kids bring home these germs and pass them on to some of the family who then pass them on to the rest. This back and forth can be an issue for moms and dads and baby brothers and sisters and anyone else in the house. The immunity will build up as your family is exposed to these new microbes, but pay attention to your health and wellness, too. Kindergarten can bring some unexpected concerns for the entire family.

Another item Not on the checklist but worth mentioning is a quick reminder about sleep and snacks. School demands lots of energy from kids. Getting enough sleep at night helps children handle the day. Fresh fruit and veggie snacks avoid sugar highs and energy spikes.

To some extent dressing independently depends on the clothes. Some zippers on coats and sweaters are tricky even for teachers, and tying shoelaces is a complicated skill that not all can do. Velcro is great for kindergarten, even if it can be a noisy distraction at quiet time but, for the most part, children need to be able to handle taking off their coats, changing shoes, putting their coats on, undoing and doing up the buttons on their pants, etc. by themselves.

There are lots of parent and teacher stories about getting kids dressed, especially in the winter, but my personal favorite has to do with Undressing. A colleague of mine said she turned around one day in her classroom to discover a little boy at the paint center quite naked. His mother had told him that if he went to the paint station to take off his sweater and not to get paint on his clothes. It was a long instruction but he did remember the first and last parts of the message…if he went to the paint center to take off blah, blah, blah, his clothes. So, that's what he did. He took off all this clothes and was quite happily painting knowing that he had done what he was told and that his clothes would be paint-free. My friend was glad that the principal hadn't chosen that moment to drop by as she explained to the student that he could use a paint shirt to protect his clothes, but he needed to wear them at school so he wasn't all naked.

The checklist I've given you covers some basics, and there are more that could be included. Under the heading of self-help skills, but not on the list, are ones like:

- Does your child feel confident enough to ask for help when needed?
- Can your child tell an adult when s/he feels sick?
- Does your child know a home phone number in case of an emergency?
- Can your child work independently for short periods of time?
- Can your child make his or her own choices?

These are also important coping skills and ones to work on with your child and there are surely more, but the checklist ones are a good place to start.

Emotional Readiness

Separating from parents or caregivers is the next checklist point. This one word, separating, can be a big deal. Some kids are so comfortable with the issue that it would maybe feel kind of nice if there was an "I'll miss you". For others, this may be a major concern. Some kids have been going to daycare for years without any problems, but suddenly, the kindergarten class door opens, the morning skips a beat and there's a flood of tears.

In general, a child that has difficulty handling even short periods of separation without trauma would rate a 1. A child that can cope with planned, brief times without someone familiar to them would rate a 2. A 3 child can usually handle saying good-bye to parents when required, be it a quick drop-off with the sitter or a whole day at daycare. Children who are confident, eager to be on their own and who may not even notice when parents go, are likely to score a 4.

As with other areas of development, separating is not always easy to assess. For a couple of years, my son didn't even call me Mom, using my first name instead. But he ran and hid in the wooden fort when I dropped him off at preschool. Sometimes, children will be quite content and independent at daycare for most of the day, but nap-time can be more of a challenge. (Ideas to help children handle separation as they start kindergarten are included at the end of this part, under FAQs.)

Another big self-help area is: Is your child aware of and able to express and regulate emotions? Afraid. Sad. Disappointed. Excited. Anxious. By this age for children,

---

there's been a lot of growth and development in this area, especially when you remember the two-year old stage. But there's considerable difference between 4-year olds and 5-year olds, too.

Here are some questions to consider:

- How does your child respond to new faces? New situations?
- How does your child cope with change?
- How does your child learn new routines?
- How does your child deal with Not being able to do what he or she wants to do?
- How self-reliant and independent is your child?

Emotional skills such as these aren't a simple yes or no, checkmark or x. Emotional growth and development are an on-going, active process. Plus, many overlap into social areas. Social and emotional aspects can be thought of as two sides of the same coin. The social side relates to interactions with others—external. The emotional side refers to understanding and controlling one's emotions—internal. There are good reasons for including emotional readiness in the section on social skills and just as valid points for mentioning it here with self-help and other self-regulation skills. No matter where they are included, emotional coping skills are sometimes *more important than any of the rest*, when it comes to readiness for any event, not just school. We will certainly be going over social skills, and expanding more on emotional aspects, in a later section.

Rating Self-help Skills and Emotional Readiness

To help your evaluation, I will describe children from each level and let you match your child to one of these. (I'll use both genders alternating each one, but meaning both.) For each section, most children will have a mixture of numbers beside the individual items as well as a general, overall level of readiness.

This is a description of a 1. A child who is not yet emotionally ready for kindergarten may be either very shy or very egocentric. The painfully shy child is reluctant to attend. His body language says I'm scared, I'm anxious. Shoulders are hunched over, head down, eyes big. He needs lots of coaxing to participate in new situations and takes a long time to warm up to new people. He clings onto caregivers, seeming lost and fearful. He needs lots of attention and direction and craves physical security.

An egocentric child may also be a 1. She finds it very difficult to cope with routines and expectations. "But I don't want to do that. I don't like it. I'm doing this." Not the anxious follower, she leads and demands that others do what she wants. In either case, there may be tears, wails and refusals. These are two very different personalities but, for both, the current emotional state and coping responses indicate a readiness concern.

Impulsiveness, that is acting without thinking is problematic before school even starts. This child is unable to self-monitor actions and appears to act without considering others or consequences. Examples of impulsive behavior include starting something without hearing all the directions, interrupting, blurting out comments, running off to get or do something, chasing, and just leaving. Sometimes, these actions create heart-stopping moments for adults.

For children like this, joining a community program, parks and recreation activities, or library story hour may be helpful to encourage skills to deal with the emotional demands of kindergarten. Self-control, independence and self-reliance are like muscles; they develop and strengthen with practice, moderate challenge and coaching.

Onto a 2. She may be timid, unsure, hangs back but the tears dry up and she reluctantly joins in after some observation. Once he feels comfortable, the situation and routine are okay, unless there is an unexpected change when more than average intervention is needed. There may be an emotional outburst or temper tantrum but with help, control is reestablished.

Assistance might take the form of modeling from a parent or other adult, "Oh, I feel really frustrated and upset when I can't do what I want, but I'll take a deep breath and let my body loosen up and feel soft and slow down and I feel better." Independence is growing for this child and a 2 may be fine with more directions, "Hmm, what do you think comes next after painting a picture? And then what? Can you tell me what comes after?" Self-reliance can be promoted, too. "You really liked hearing this story. For a few minutes, look at the pages by yourself and check if you can remember what happens." Intervention and support help develop emotional readiness skills.

Description of a 3. This child handles most situations, except the really scary or unusual ones. He may not like when there's a whole great big group but copes by finding a friend and feels more secure. She may choose to sit close to the teacher or another adult and observes others carefully, watching for their reactions as she sorts out her own. Reminders usually suffice for misbehaviors.

By and large, these kidlets are comfortable in new situations and deal with their own emotions. Interventions may occasionally be needed, but redirections are usually enough. A smile, a wink to acknowledge their needs and they are fine. Maybe a question, "Could it be you need some attention for a minute? Could it be that you are anxious right now?" Generally, independence and self-reliance are evident. He can make choices about what to work and play with and accesses materials independently. She figures out if is she is cold and goes to get a sweater without needing an adult. Support is not needed constantly as with a 1, or close monitoring as with a 2. Periodic help is enough for a 3.

Lastly, a 4. Emotionally stable and aware, these children may even notice emotional needs in others. He may ask a friend, "Are you sad today? Want to come sit with me and look at this?" She may even help her friend approach an adult with a concern, "There's a problem with the snack. My friend needs help."

These independent and self-reliant children have less obvious emotional needs and we need to remember to give them recognition and not just take them for granted.

Again, these evaluations are just tools. In some situations, some 3-level children may have a 1 or 2 reaction, or even a very withdrawn child may be surprisingly emotionally empathetic for a special friend or younger sibling. But, using this tool as an overall quick snapshot, how do you evaluate your child's emotional readiness? 1, 2, 3 or 4. Confidence, assurance, independence, feelings of self-worth and empowerment are really important, especially if a person is only 5 years old.

Here are some Frequently Asked Questions that target the area of self-help skills.

My child can't tie his shoes. What can I do?

Step-by-step, practice one area at a time. Use two different colors of laces. Knot them together at one end as if they were one big long lace and lace the shoe. As you get to the top one color is on one side and one on the other. It's much easier to practice with two different colors. At school, I break the task into several steps and work on only one step at a time. First, we practice making the x or crossing over and under and pulling tight. Then, the bunny ears and loop. No matter which method you use for tying laces, segment the process—small steps, one part at a time.

My child can't yet print her name. Are there activities that will help?

While this isn't really a self-help skill, it does seem to fit in here. At school, the teacher will usually use your child's first name. If you have been using a family nickname, help your child become familiar with her first name, too. Practice printing upper case for initial letter and lower case for the others. Roll them with play-dough, color on the driveway with sidewalk chalk, trace them in the sandbox, squeeze them on the dinner plate with ketchup, drizzle them with syrup on pancakes at breakfast. Once at school, she'll write them often.

My child is nervous about starting school. How can we handle THE FIRST DAY?

No matter whether you have rated your child a 1,2,3, or 4 for emotional readiness and separating from parents and caregivers, some discussion beforehand helps. If possible, visit the school and talk about the first day. Perhaps, say something like this: "You know, sometimes when I think of you going to kindergarten, I'm a little sad. I think I will miss you, a little bit. This is something new for you to do by yourself. And sometimes, when I think of you going to kindergarten, I'm very excited. You will be doing new things, and making new friends and learning new things. I feel a little sad and a little excited at the same time." Then, ask your child about his or her feelings and ideas of what kindergarten is all about. We might think it is obvious that "Kindergarten is when little kids go to school", but children often have different answers:

It's important to let your child know that ambivalent feelings are OK, that he or she may be excited and scared at the same time. There may be tears, little people ones and big people ones, too. Maybe there will be so many that puddles will grow and grow until they are big enough to wash cars. But, after all, you will see each other soon so it's okay if the sun dries up the puddles and the tears.

It may help to act out each step beforehand. Go to the steps of the school and let your child practice blowing kisses and telling you good-bye. Then, switch roles and let your child be the parent and you be the child, but vary your responses; cry and whimper, wail loudly, whine, have fun and hopefully, at some point, your child will giggle and tell you how silly you are. Then, ask your child if s/he thinks it's okay now.

Talk about specifics. Ask your child what he could do if he had to go to the bathroom. Or, what she could do if she didn't know something or didn't like her snack. Let your child think of some solutions, and then say you think some of those ideas are pretty good, alright, and maybe things won't always be fine, but ideas like that show that his or her brain is working and will help figure things out.

Have fun with some bizarre ideas, what if the walls turned to chocolate and melted when the sun came out? What if the teacher turned into a bag of popcorn? Let your child imagine and talk while you listen carefully. Hidden in some of the 'what if's' might be a kernel of the things that are really underneath the anxiety. (Pardon the pun. That's one of the other advantages of teaching young children, or disadvantages from my family's point of view, a rather quirky sense of humor that pops up all the time. It's become somewhat ingrained. Ha, ha.)

Reassure your child about kindergarten and, at the same time, let your child know that you are confident in him or her, too. "Yeah, sometimes when I think about it I'm a little sad, and a little excited. But I know I can handle that, and I know you can, too. We'll handle this together even when we are apart."

It's especially hard to leave when your little one is crying. Often, long good-byes can actually be harder on your child than short ones. Saying something like the following, in a matter-of-fact voice with a business-like tone, "I see that you are upset. You might feel like crying for a little while so here's a kiss to hold in your hand. It's time for me to go, now. I'll see you at home," acknowledges the feeling. Doing this may feel like your heart is being ripped out. But, at the same time, it conveys to your child that you are confident and comfortable and expect that s/he will feel like that, too.

Supplied with confidence, some basic school tools and lots of hugs and kisses, you will both be ready for the journey and adventure.

Info to find out for First Day:

- where do we go?
- do we line-up?
- what time do parents come with kids?
- do they need a snack?
- any supplies for first day?
- do we stay with the kids or go and come back?
- when do we pick them up?
- WHERE DO WE PICK THEM UP?

Other information you'll need may include:

- what supplies are needed?
- is there an additional fee?
- kinds of snacks?
- what about being late for drop-off or pick-up?
- what happens on birthdays? and field trips?
- what communication comes home?
- emergencies?
- schedule? classroom volunteering?

Supplies Usually Needed:

- simple backpack large enough for books,
- ziplock back of extra old clothes, gym-time non-slip runners,
- non-allergy self-contained snack like an apple or banana (just in case),
- sheet of paper for the always-hungry paper monster that lives in the backpack and eats notices so he doesn't eat any Start-up Information Notes from today!

How can I make the "drop off" easier for us both?

In the event your child is having continued difficulty after the First Day, (see the part before this one for First Day separation ideas), I'm going to use that same answer I gave about learning to tie shoes: Practice. Go to the parking lot. "Here we are at school, this is how it works." Run through the drill, then go get a treat, like a popsicle. Do this a few different times. If you need to, choose to practice at a really inconvenient time for your child—to the point of having to skip doing something fun for practice time. Generate some complaining. Then ask, "Are you sure that's enough? Well, when it really happens maybe you will cry, and maybe you will be upset. Maybe we should do this 5 more times, 10 more, 30 more?" Finally, your child in exasperation says, "I'll be fine." You may hesitate and waffle but you should get the desired "I'll be fine," response, although the tone probably won't be. You might say, "Ok, ok, but if you change your mind and are sad, then we'll practice again. Even after the next time at school, I won't be able to practice right away, but maybe on the weekend, instead of doing — ". That way, if drop-off is a problem, you are not threatening to skip something fun, you are working your hardest to help your child deal with the problem. It's gone from a power struggle to a team working to figure things out.

Well, let's go back to those three questions
that are keeping us on track.

How do I know if
my child is ready
for kindergarten?

What does my child
need to learn before
kindergarten?

How do I best get my
child ready and provide
ongoing support?

Recap: Here is a recap of self-help and emotional readiness: By kindergarten, children should be fairly independent. Check and make sure that your little boy knows how to use urinals. Other than that, children of both sexes should be able to take care of going to the bathroom, wiping if needed, wrestling with their clothes, and washing and drying their hands. Flushing and hands often need reminders. (Kindergarten can be a challenge for your health, too.)

Children need to be mostly able to take care of their own clothing and their own needs. The biggies when it comes to self-help skills are self-reliance and independence. For instance, is your child able to work and play on his or her own, able to separate and stay at school without mom or dad or another caregiver, and able to ask for a drink or to use the restroom? Being able to make choices and follow the routines, being able to deal with changes in routines and unexpected events are also self-help skills.

Emotional readiness deals with how your child feels internally with the issue of going off to school. A 1 child feels very fearful, reluctant, and has anxieties about lots of little things or is still very-centered on his or her own needs and demands lots of attention. Some children just want to play and do their own thing and are not ready to accommodate and work as part of a group. A 2 looks somewhat similar, although you can see some growing independence and self-reliance. Two-year olds can be terribly independent but by the age of 5, most children accept that adults can help and can ask for help if needed, but want to assume more responsibility for their needs. Evaluating or assigning a number isn't cut and dried, so it doesn't matter so much if you give your child a 1 or a 2.

What's important is that you note that this is an area that looks like some support would be beneficial. Being able to respond to new faces and new situations with adequate confidence and assurance, ready to balance some work and play would indicate a 3 or a 4, a child who is comfortable and reasonably content.

We've gone over one aspect of kindergarten readiness, that of self-skills and emotional readiness. You have used an evaluation tool to assess privately, for yourself, your child's readiness. Did you mark down a 1,2,3, or 4 next to each question in this section of the checklist? You can now look and see what areas need support before kindergarten and you have some ideas of ways to provide that support and strategies to prepare your child for the first day.

Next stop, communication skills.

Q. What do you get when you cross a parrot
and a centipede?
A. A walky-talky.

Q. What do skeletons use to communicate?
A. Cellbones.

Chapter Two
C = Communication and Language

Communication and Language Readiness Skills

The objective in this part is to go over communication and language readiness. There are four points on the checklist, and these are: speaks understandably in 5-6 word sentences, responds to basic requests, follows 2-part directions, and draws pretend word scribbles or letter strings. As before, more skills could be included but these give you a general idea.

A scale of 1,2,3, or 4 is being used to evaluate development and readiness. A number 1 indicates a skill that is not yet developed. 2 is a skill that is developing but not yet all that comfortable or consistent for the child. 3 is a skill that is comfortable and evident most of the time. 4 is a skill that is well developed and the child is ready to go on to the next level. Just in case numbers are flashing across your mind, giving your child 1's and 2's is not a panic situation. It indicates that your child could benefit from some extra time and attention to some of these issues. (See section A for checklist and evaluation descriptors.)

In a typical kindergarten class, there are indeed some children who have speech issues. As a teacher, every year I ask our school's speech and language pathologist to do some further testing, and she sends us the results. Sometimes, she says, "Let's just watch this child, I think this is an area that will continue to develop and catch-up on it's own." Sometimes, she recommends intervention for correcting tongue thrusts or consonant blends or lisping or stuttering and sees a child once or twice a week for a term or over the course of the year, or perhaps, for as much as two or three years. Sometimes the parents are aware there is a concern and ask about testing, sometimes not. If testing is needed, most schools require that parents give their permission, although some basic screening is usually allowed just to see if there is a need for more assessment.

Language issues are more difficult and occasionally some children require longer term or more intense intervention and support, but usually these are children that are already in a program, in which case it's the school that's receiving the information and the parent who is giving it.

Typically, a five-year-old child is correctly using most plurals and past tenses. No longer "mans" and "foots", but "men" and "feet," although not cacti or fungi. She "getted" a book and he "goed" to the store is now she got and he went. Most of the everyday place words are used, such as: in, on, under, over, inside, outside, top and bottom. Several more are understood: underneath, overhead, below, beneath. Also, most five-year olds can compare and say if something is longer, or shorter than something else. Common opposites: big-little, hard-soft, heavy-light, up-down, are also used correctly. They can also identify 6+ colors.

Concepts of time are evident, such as morning, afternoon, night, day, later, before, and after. However, before and after may be switched especially when an adult is asking for the order as to how something happened. She hit me first after I hit her. At school, we work on Tomorrow and Yesterday, but Today seems understood.

The important body parts are named, some more accurately than others. Most familiar animals are correctly identified, too, as are everyday objects, and pictures in books or magazines. I remember one student that raised some concerns one year calling a feather a bird-leaf. That took some thinking to connect the object with the source, the feather to the bird, and relate the shape to something similar, a leaf, which also falls, but it did show that language was not typical.

Sentences should be fairly long, 5-6+ words, with a few being even more complex. Some children are naturally more verbal than others. One child might simply say, "Mom, you forgot to pack my snack," and another, "Mom, you forgot to pack my snack and I was starving and nobody would share and I know we are having fish for supper and I don't like it and I'm going to Grandma's house," but both are typical of five-year olds. One has a longer word count but it's just sentences strung together with ands. (At the teenage stage sentences collapse.)

When explaining something, or pretending something, there may be a lot of repetition and lots of he's and she's so it's hard to know who did what, but one can usually figure it out, and on the whole, the speaking is grammatically correct. A few adverbs and adjectives are used, too: really, really fast, monster-size, teeny-tiny, gross, etc.

Most speech sounds are there, all the vowel (a-e-i-o-u) sounds and most of the consonants (b, d, f, g, h, j, k, m, n, p, s, t, v, w, y, and z). The l's and r's may be developed or still developing, also the combinations such as sh or ch. That's fairly common. But speech should be understandable by non-family members despite a few articulation problems.

Your son or daughter should understand most simple questions and can reply to requests. If a question contains an A or B choice, many young children will choose the B, just because it is last. For instance, the question "Do you want a stuffie or a book?" will prompt the book choice. Teachers have to watch for this when testing. "Is this wheel a square or a circle?" The child may get the correct answer just because of the way the question was worded.

Following directions, or rather, not following directions may have an underlying issue of willingness, but children should be able to comply with 2 instructions given at one time. "Hang up your coat and put away your toy," or "Wash your hands and get a book," have 2 parts in the instruction. At this age, children can usually remember and act on both parts without one over-riding the other.

Another consideration is how your child uses language. Does he use language to ask for things or to tell you what's happened? Can she respond to suggestions such as, "Let's play with blocks," with a different idea if she wants? Do you need to use lots of prompts and questions to encourage your child to talk, or have you the opposite concern? When your child tells you a story about an event is his voice flat and unemotional, just listing details? How about when you say no, does she attempt to persuade you by using some emotion in her voice, some idea as to what she's feeling in her use of language? Connecting feelings, events, purpose, and vocabulary requires some heavy-duty thinking skills but this is profoundly important in relating to the world and others. No wonder children need lots of opportunities to use language as they work and play.

Communication is more than just language: there is context and how one says something. Children often find relating an event much easier if they can reenact it, supplying the context at the same time. So, telling about going to the playground is accompanied by all the actions, too. And if there was a painful tumble off the slide in the morning, the tears resurface when telling about it at supper. All these things are considerations, too, even if they are not covered by a checklist.

Language and communication are not limited to the words being spoken. There's also the visual or written aspect. Some children are experimenting with writing, such as strings of letters, often just capital or upper-case letters. They may notice signs, advertisements, and things that start with the same letter as their name. And some children are not yet interested.

Rating Communication and Language Readiness

Beside communication and language mark a 1-4. As in the first section (B), there could be varying numbers for each point. Usually, there is one number that indicates a predominant level of readiness despite the differences.

For a 1 rating, language is a definite concern and may indicate a strong need for additional speech and language support. This child is difficult to understand and struggles to find the right words. There may also be little awareness of and experimentation with written communication.

A 2 child can sometimes be difficult to understand and you may have noticed language that lags behind other kids. There are a few early attempts to write, such as printing a name. Speech and language support may again be needed as well as lots of stimulation in the target language.

Language is fine for a child at the 3 level, maybe missing some of the harder speech sounds like the r. There is an interest in early writing, such as upper-case letter strings when playing, in printing MOM or DAD or other names, or copying words.

A child who uses language effectively and has an amazing vocabulary, especially when arguing, even talks for the other kids in the family, and tells way too much to visitors, would typically describe a 4. Some children at the 4 level may be primarily verbal and show little interest in anything to do with writing.

Isn't it amazing how we can notice, already at this early age, some children who, as adults, would not be best suited to jobs where they would have to write tons of reports? We can predict that some will not be as happy in the front office meeting clients as they will be behind the scenes. How much or how little your child talks may be a reflection of personality and your own family. There is a wide range in normal language development. Nevertheless, there is no doubt that language is used for learning and we need to nourish early language skills.

Here are some ways that parents can support communication and language development, both spoken and written, before, during, and after, kindergarten (and promote learning to read, too).

In addition to reading books and telling stories to children, there are lots of language activities that will enhance readiness. Although it sounds simple and can be summed up in one sentence, it is tremendously important: *Immerse your child in a language bath.* (By the way, this is the best advice for learning another language, too.)

Not only does this language bath help for communicating, it helps children develop the tools they will need for mastering reading. Research has found that one simple aspect of using language is highly related to learning to read. What is it? The ability to use rhymes. *Rhyming.* If your child can give you a word that sounds like another, s/he has an important skill for reading. It's called phonological awareness and refers to the ability to separate words into their sound parts and to manipulate them. So bat becomes 'buh' and 'at' and the 'at' can be recombined to be 'mmm + at' or mat. Now, it's easier to see why this is so important for reading.

When you are reading or telling a story with words that rhyme, stop and have your child think of what that word could be. Rhyming games are fun anytime and anywhere. (P.S. Especially if grandma and grandpa are present, do not mindlessly use the word *truck* as a clue. You will never be able to forget it, because someone in the family will always say, "Do you remember when you…?" Also, it isn't advisable to say the darn car won't *start*. Instead of getting any assistance, one ends up with a spousal lecture on appropriate things to teach the kids just because a small voice in the backseat has said, "Hey, that rhymes with f…"!)

This language bath to support language and communication development can take place all over the house. Because we spend so much time in the kitchen on a daily basis, let's start there.

Doing the dishes: Washing dishes or loading the dishwasher is a good time to name the utensils and talk about them. You might say, "These 2 spoons aren't the same size. Look, they are different." Then, talk about why the soup spoon is bigger than the dessert spoon. Make up a story about a house where the dessert spoon was bigger than the soup spoon and what happened at mealtimes, maybe it was as big as a cup on a stick. Ask the plate what it most likes served on it at supper, then use a plate-sounding voice and tell all about it. Have your child choose another plate and have a conversation, "Ooh, I love spaghetti, all that gooey, thick, red sauce. But I'm not sure about broccoli. It looks like baby trees so maybe I'll eat it. A tree on a plate. Pretty big plate. How about you yellow plate? Do you only eat yellow food?"

Books often use dialogue in the story line and having this experience helps for reading. Having an activity like this is a good back-up plan in case there is a starving appetite at the table and you need a few more minutes. It also makes clean-up a lot more fun when the dishes are talking to you or each other.

Food Prep: Vegetables and fruits have wonderful colors and shapes and sizes and textures and flavors to talk about. Just think of all that vocabulary and rich language. What did the apple say to the orange? What did the apple say to the slicer? Talk about the tools in the kitchen. Get their names mixed up. "Please pass me the egg-beater so I can open this can. No, no the egg-beater. I'm trying to open this can, I need the egg-beater. Please pass me the egg-beater, why do you keep passing me this funny-looking windmill?" Your child will so enjoy being able to tell you the correct name. This gives kids a chance to exercise not just their language and communication abilities, but the imagination muscles, too.

Plus, there are all the skills that go into explaining how to cook something, and what we have to do and how to figure things out. Talk about personal likes and dislikes. These days children are exposed to so many different kinds of things, it's a great opportunity to talk about why families eat different kinds of foods.

Recipes: Using a recipe to make something models the importance of written communication. Some cooking books have great pictures and are motivating just to look at. Recipes can be turned into pictures on a paper or little dry erase board so your child can help you read them. Pictures of a big cup of juice, a banana and a mixer are easily readable to follow along and make a smoothie. Have your child draw the picture of the finished smoothie, with a big smiley ☺.

Grocery Shopping: Getting the groceries is also a great time for using language. Make a list to take to the store in words and pictures so the kids can help you read it. If you have time, just to keep the kids off-balance—after all, they keep us off-balance—instead of saying no when they want something stop and challenge them to give you 5 good reasons as to why you should buy it.
(Another P.S. A few times, my own children were so convincing, though, that I had to buy the item, but on the condition that they never, ever told their mother about it. Never, ever would she be able to tolerate such behavior in

herself as to allow her children to consume that product. And I would leave, tsking and shaking my head while they giggled and shushed. Pretending that I was someone other than 'Mom' for just those few minutes gave me the space to alter a rule that I would otherwise maintain so that I could be consistent. I admit that it's fancy footwork.) At some point, your children may supply you with a list of dos and don'ts if they have to go shopping with you, but at the age of 5, you still have lots of time. Since we have to go shopping, I don't see why we can't enjoy the job.

Okay, out of the kitchen and into the rest of the house.

Laundry Time: Laundry is another task that needs a dose of fun and language can supply it. Make groups and sort the clothes according to their category, "These are towels, these are sheets." Compare the sizes, shapes, colors, and textures, here, too. Sometimes children can put items into a correct group but not always give the category a name. Pick out a sock and be its voice as it says, "Oh, you wouldn't believe where I went today. I walked and walked all the way to — . And then I had to — ". Laundry can be a lot less boring as you help your child develop and use language.

As you put away the clean clothes, it's a great time to practice prepositions, "These go in the drawer, under the whatevers, not on top, and just beside these." Having your child draw pictures and label the drawers can be a fun, rainy day activity. One can even instruct the clothes to stay clean because they are travelling to the laundry room much too often or, should you find them on the floor, lecture the clothes.

Believe me, even teenagers will hustle their laundry into the hampers with the offer that maybe their clothes need another stern talking-to, with the hint that you may do so within a friend's hearing. Exasperation caused by a well-meaning and totally innocent parent is really quite effective. (Caution: hearing your son lecturing the car about getting home so late after curfew when he'd told it repeatedly that it needed to come home may indicate the need for a new language strategy!)

Language with a Vacuum: Other rooms in the house lend themselves to developing vocabulary about spaces and spatial relationships: farther, closer, beside, behind, in front of, etc. Vacuuming has never been high on my fun things to do list, but the task can be a little more fun if you have your child give you directions of where to vacuum. "Go three steps straight ahead and vacuum behind the sofa; turn to the left and vacuum underneath the big chair," and so on. You may be able to give him or her a turn to run the vacuum, while you give the directions. (Sneaky, but clever!)

Speaking of directions, your child may not yet always use left and right accurately. In kindergarten, when singing some songs such as hokey-pokey, I will occasionally put a stamp on the right hand so it can go in and out and is easy to tell from the left. There is new research that indicates some differences between the male brain and the female brain with regards to spatial awareness and left-right directions. You may have noticed this in your house, and not only with the kids.

Signs Language: Various signs can be made throughout the house, such as "Sit Here", and then when memorized and understood moved from the chair to the fridge for reading humor. Words can come later, after drawings, squiggles or pictures. These can be drawn or cut out from newspapers and magazines.

Draw pictures and send squiggle letters to family and friends across the country or across town. Everyone loves to get mail. (Do you think there's a chance that if we start kids using electronic communication technology, i.e. email, Facebook, Twitter, now, at the preschool stage that they will rebel and be less enamored with it when they are teenagers? Reverse psychology, maybe?)

In the part on pre-academic issues, there will be more information about sounds, and letters, and making those connections but I'm sure you have some ideas about how to encourage and support language and communication development. The demands on kids for acquiring and storing knowledge and information seem to be increasing, so much so that children will need parent help all through school.

All these language activities can be done at the same time as you are doing other things. Instead of increasing the load on your energy by planning separate learning exercises, you can turn mundane, ordinary jobs into fun sharing times, with lots of laughter and silliness. In fact, this seems to lighten the load.

Children have practiced giving you reasons why; they know sometimes you will say no and sometimes yes. Plus, if your children have had lots of practice talking and communicating with you it does pay off in later years when there are challenges and talking together is not so much fun. As a parenting columnist, Judith Wood says, "Parenting isn't a science and it isn't an art. It's a fudge."

How do I know if
my child is ready
for kindergarten?

What does my child
need to learn before
kindergarten?

How do I best get my
child ready and provide
ongoing support?

Sum-up: To summarize, in children of kindergarten age speech should be understandable and grammatically correct. Rhyming is an important skill. Most sounds have developed, r being one of the last, along with some sound blends. Spoken language is both understood and used to meet needs. There are lots of ways to use and promote language and communication by piggy-backing onto things you already do. The next part is social readiness, how your child relates to others and copes in a group.

Chapter Three
D = Do you want to be my friend?
Social (and Emotional) Issues

Social and Emotional Readiness Skills

Social and emotional development can be thought of as two sides of the same coin. Emotional development is internal, involving feelings and thoughts. Social development is external, dealing with how we relate to others. As mentioned in the introduction, going off to kindergarten is a new, unexplored territory for a child, just as going off to a new, foreign country is for you. Even if the language hasn't changed the dynamics have. As if that wasn't enough, there's some kind of numbers game going on! Instead of 1 or 2 adults and one five-year old with a couple brothers or sisters, there are now 15 to 25 four and five-year olds and 1 adult, possibly 2. How you cope with all these challenges will significantly affect your thoughts and feelings. These, in turn, will affect how you relate to all these new people and your new surroundings.

Dealing with these challenges is a pretty big job; it demands lots of energy and support. No wonder our kidlets sometimes get cranky or demanding or clingy. Just because a person is only 1 or 2 or 3 or 4 or 5 years old, doesn't mean life is simple and uncomplicated. It only looks that way from the outside. Nonetheless, by the age of five, children have developed some basic social skills. For the most part, they enjoy playing with others of the same age, are able to share and play together and are comfortable in small groups of peers. We'll expand on these abilities as we talk about the levels.

Rating Social and Emotional Readiness

Level 3: Starting with level 3, here are both an overview of average five-year-old social development and some descriptors. Let's imagine some typical five-year old children, either boys or girls, with birth dates in any part of the year.

In general, he likes playing with others and can control aggressive impulses, at least most of the time. She doesn't need to use hitting, kicking, biting, or verbal aggression, such as name-calling or threats when playing with peers, usually. He takes turns and can share with others. She can share the attention of adults or friends in the group. He uses please and thank you and other basic good manners. She may even approach others and invite them to play.

Five-year olds are often kind and helpful. They like to tell jokes and share laughter with others, although the punch line doesn't necessarily relate to the rest of the joke, and the oddest things can be funny. Sometimes to get attention he tries out bathroom or swear words. She can also be bossy as she tries out leadership skills. Generally, he likes to make his own decisions and she is comfortable taking a few risks.

Five-year olds like to test their abilities, sometimes even boast about them but they are not yet ready for competition on an emotional level, even though they will engage each other in contests. "I can drink faster than you can, jump higher, burp louder, walk slower." The list seems endless.

Although becoming more sensitive to the feelings of others, they may still exclude playmates from their clubs. With a basic and developing understanding of right and wrong and a growing respect for rules, five year olds invent rules and conditions in their play. Sometimes he may be critical of others and embarrassed when he makes a mistake. Able to carry on conversations, she may be reluctant to express feelings.

Children at this age like adult approval and often check for permission to do things. At the same time, they can work and play independently without constant adult supervision. They engage in both giving and receiving behaviors and often enjoy collecting things. Play-time is a mixture of fantasy and reality, the everyday and the far out.

Five-year olds like to seem grown-up but may still fear loud noises, the dark or animals. They have enough confidence to separate from their parents. For children at this age, because their world is expanding so much and so quickly, routines and rules offer a sense of stability and security. Limits and boundaries keep things in their world from getting too confusing, even though children test and push against them.

By this stage of the game (pardon the pun) children have progressed through several stages of play. The first stage of play is solitary-play then parallel-play. Think of the two parallel lines of a railroad track; they are in the same area, close together, but have limited interacting. Associative play follows this: sharing materials and activities, some interactions but loosely organized. A leader may emerge with other children as followers. Co-operative play is just that: an exchange of ideas, sharing of materials and roles, along with a shared aim or purpose. While children will play at various levels at different times in kindergarten, co-operative play is emerging and becoming common.

This is an overview of average five-year-old social development. If the above describes your son or daughter most of the time, you could feel comfortable writing a 3 for social readiness.

Level 1: A child who questions rules constantly, needs lots of adult attention, and has difficulty working independently, is much less ready for kindergarten. This child may also challenge peers when playing and is engaged primarily in solitary or only parallel play. He can't wait for turns, solves problems with impulsive or aggressive choices and takes little responsibility for these choices. She has difficulty separating from parents or caregivers and shows little awareness of others' feelings.

Level 2: A child who has some of these challenges and shows readiness in a few areas would be a 2.

Level 4: A 4 child relates well with peers and adults, is self-confident and assured in small and large groups, and is empathetic and mannerly. S/he has lucky and no doubt, grateful and happy, parents.

These previous paragraphs answered our first two questions, HOW DO I KNOW IF MY CHILD IS READY socially FOR KINDERGARTEN? WHAT DOES MY CHILD NEED TO LEARN socially BEFORE KINDERGARTEN? So, onto the third, HOW DO I BEST GET MY CHILD READY AND PROVIDE ONGOING SUPPORT in terms of social readiness? This third question is certainly the most difficult of the three, and social/ emotional readiness the most difficult of all the aspects of development. While social skills *seem* to evolve naturally, they require a great deal of nurturing and time on the part of parents and caregivers, and teachers, for that matter. All too often, academic preparedness seems to overshadow the critical importance of social and emotional readiness. (That's why the B,C,D,E and A order in the Table of Contents, Part One.)

Here are a few suggestions to promote social and emotional growth and development.

Talking: Very young children react quickly to their emotions and social situations. As children grow and develop, this gives way to thinking and talking about their feelings and making choices about how to respond. About this age, children can accept mixed emotions and understand how people can have very different emotions to the same situation. Labeling or talking about an emotion shifts it to a different area of the brain. This helps create a space between feeling and acting, giving time to choose an action rather than just reacting.

Books: Books and stories are a great help in giving a framework to talk about how people are feeling, why they acted how they did, discussing better choices, and just providing and expanding vocabulary for lots of different emotions. These books and stories help develop perspective and the ability to see things from someone else's point of view which is part of empathy. Using emotions in play activities gives children opportunities to practice facial expressions, voice tones and body positions for different emotions, as well as problem-solving and exploring different responses.

One of the stories I often use is one you might remember, Where the Wild Things Are by Maurice Sendak. We talk about Max's wild behavior, the consequence of going to his room without any supper, the wild rumpus—could this possibly be how Max feels inside, like there are monsters right inside him, not just his bedroom?—and to feeling lonely and coming home. What happens when everything, that is the feelings inside Max, are calm? There's his supper and it's still hot. Any library or bookstore will have lots more ideas for books to promote social-emotional development.

Games and Pretend: Games such as Simon Says, Freeze Tag, Red Light-Green Light, and Statues help children practice control of their bodies. During physical activities, have your child feel how fast his heart is beating or notice how quickly she needs to breathe. Just after having a quiet snuggle, check those again so your child has a body-experience and vocabulary for feeling quiet, calm and relaxed. Pretending to feel angry, sad, scared, worried, disappointed, and other emotions are also ways to help your child become aware of how his or her body responds and reacts. Silly games are fun ways to learn, too: "When I eat pizza, I feel really, really, really scared. Those triangle pieces are the same shape as teeth and maybe they will eat me all up. Oh, no, no, what can I do? Maybe I will have to count backwards." This stimulates lots of discussion about what things are scary and what things help. "When I eat ice cream, I feel really, really, really sad. I eat the ice cream and it melts and turns into tears and then I cry. Do you get sad when you eat ice cream? No? Well, when do you feel sad?" Even reluctant, quiet children feel safe talking about emotions when the atmosphere is so non-threatening.

Songs: The song, If You're Happy and You Know it, can have endless verses for checking out facial expressions and learning how to read them on others: "If you're happy and you know it, make that face. If you're sad and you know it, make that face, boo-hoo. If you're mad and you know it, then your face is going to show it, if you're scared and you know it make that face."

Toys: Toys can be drafted as players in social stories: "Now, listen, Truck, it's okay to be upset with the cars when they are using the whole track and there's no room for you. It's not okay to push them out of the way. Let's try asking: Hey there cars. I'd like to play, too. There's no room for me. I need a little space."

Be the voice of a sad and lonely ball that wants a friend to play with but doesn't know how to ask. Help it discover some ways to invite others to play. Voice the request of the toy box as it says: "Toys, toys, it's time to come home, now. It's not being very considerate of others to just spread yourselves all over the floor. Somebody has to pick you up because it's not safe like that. I need you to pop yourselves right back in here, lickety split. Hop, jump and skip, 1, 2, 3, into the arms of me, thee Toy Box, and I will hug you all night long." You have reinforced a social skill, encouraged empathy, and had fun.

You've modeled a creative way to solve a problem and practiced the "I" message—that I need you to get back here. Plus, you've accomplished a needed task. You just have to get over the idea that some unenlightened adult may hear you talking like this and will wonder about your sanity.

If you can't find a book or story that helps you teach an idea to your child, just have a conversation between a couple of toys. Or if you need to do it at the dinner table, even a fork and spoon can dialogue: "My goodness, Fork, I really liked how you said please when you wanted more spaghetti." "Why thank you, Spoon. Thank you very much." "You're welcome. Would you like a little more?"

Modeling: At school, for the child who is experiencing lots of social challenges, kindergarten is not the same happy space that it is for others. As a teacher, it is important for me to be consistent with rules and routines and to give clear and simple expectations: "It's okay to be mad, it's not okay to hit," or "I can not let you chase in here, it's not safe." I take extra time to encourage independence and positive behavior choices. I may enlist the help of someone to come in at play-time, such as the school counselor or behavior support teacher, who can model sharing and negotiating skills for this child. And, I will model choosing appropriate actions to my feelings, for example: "I feel really mad that we can't go to the gym, right now. It's our turn, sigh, but another class needs it. I will take a deep breath and remember that I have lots of friends in that class and sometimes I do nice things for other people. There, the angry tight twists in my tummy are going down and my head isn't buzzing anymore."

As a parent, modeling is an effective strategy for you to use too to provide social support for your child. Use two different voices to model how to share a cookie: "I see a cookie. I'm going to eat it all up. Oh, no. That would mean there is none for you. Would you like some?" Switch voices and reply: "Oh, yes please. That is very polite for you to ask me. I like when we share." Now, you can cut the cookie in three. One piece for your child and two pieces for each of your voices. (Smart cookies will catch on that you got two pieces, but the strategy works. In desperation, modeling the right answer may help a spouse out of a conundrum.)

Academic issues may need to take a back-seat temporarily. Early on in the kindergarten year, I would no doubt communicate with the family and see how we can work on these concerns together as a team. Sometimes we discuss if waiting another year for kindergarten is the best choice, taking into account birth date, as well as what kinds of support are available during the extra year to promote social readiness. I can say that for some children waiting a year has been beneficial where the family has been able to access some programs such as parent participation pre-schools or other community resources. On occasion, the school team has also recommended two years in kindergarten to give a child more support and more time to develop these skills. Children's challenges coping socially and emotionally is the area where I, myself, most often, seek assistance and further evaluation from other in-school professionals.

There's so much research now on the crucial importance of social competence and emotional IQ. Often, I will go to a conference, seminar, or workshop, and come back to school feeling inadequate because there's another task I've heard about that I'm not doing in the classroom. Then I listen to the news or read the paper and at nearly every single headline I tkink that's a social issue, a social problem, a social concern. I repeat to myself, "Everything we need to know we learned in kindergarten. Everything we need to know we learned in kindergarten." I feel comforted and do not neglect teaching and supporting social lessons. As you can tell, this is one of the issues about which I feel most strongly. And most grateful that I am teaching five-year olds who are such eager social beings.

Wrap-up: Wrapping up this part: social readiness also involves emotional development. At this age, children enjoy playing with peers. This play is becoming more co-operative and organized. Children are increasing their range of emotions and they need to learn new vocabulary to express their thoughts and feelings. They are becoming more aware of—and more sensitive to—the feelings of other people. They are more capable of choosing their responses to others, rather than just reacting. Adults can use books, stories, songs, games, discussions, and modeling to support social-emotional readiness for kindergarten. Social-emotional development is a critically important aspect of readiness.

We've explored three areas of readiness, self-help skills, language and communication, and social-emotional aspects. Physical and motor development is coming up next and then pre-academic skills. Our three questions are keeping us on the right road:

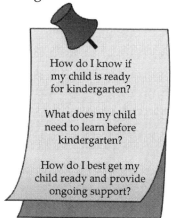

How do I know if my child is ready for kindergarten?

What does my child need to learn before kindergarten?

How do I best get my child ready and provide ongoing support?

Chapter Four
E = Exercises and Activities to Develop Physical Coordination and Abilities

Physical Development Skills and Rating

Physical or motor co-ordination can be divided into two parts, large and small muscles. These are sometimes known as gross and fine motor co-ordination. Gross motor skills or large muscle development includes big actions involving most of the body such as walking, hopping, running, throwing, and so on. Small muscle or fine motor skills are more specific actions such as pinching, fitting in puzzle pieces, coloring, cutting, etc. At this age, co-ordination and muscles are developing so physical activities for gross and fine motor co-ordination are really important.

As with all the other aspects, among children at this age, there is a considerable variation in development. Because these are specific skills, it is easy to evaluate each one using the 1,2,3,4 system. If your child can do this most of the time, mark a 3 or perhaps a 4, if it seems well mastered to you. Write in a 2 for a skill that your child can do some of the time and a 1 for a skill that has not yet developed.

Most children can hop on one foot and enjoy doing it. Any old excuse will do, having only one shoe on, a sock with two drops of water, a bumped toe or, if necessary, an imagined injury. In addition to hopping either foot can be used to balance for 5-10 seconds. Sometimes one foot may be a little easier than the other.

Jumping is another gratifying activity, with or without parental permission. Kids jump off beds, onto spongy mats, down steps, off furniture, and even from considerable heights much to parents', caregivers', and teachers' dismay. Also, they jump over things; smaller siblings, stools, line-ups of toys, block towers, or sleeping pets can all be used. (Just in case no one has ever mentioned this to you before, five-year olds have amazing energy and like to be active!)

Going down stairs alternating feet requires shifting weight and balance, but most children have developed this motor control.

Five-year-olds also delight in running, at various speeds and places, being able to stop when necessary. Running usually comes with variations on a theme such as galloping, running on tiptoes, running and jumping, running and tumbling, and other tricks. Capable of learning quite complex body co-ordination skills, children can swim, skate, dance, do gymnastics, and ride bicycles. Many of them love to perform and show what they can do. Throwing, catching, and bouncing balls are skills that are developing. Plus, these involve the added dimension of eye-hand co-ordination which is particularly important in both large and small muscle skills.

Not being able to walk or run, without bumping into walls and doorways or tripping, can be a concern. Some children choose to hit the walls or fall over furniture because they seek the extra stimulation and the excuses to move their body. Or there may be a vision problem or developmental delay. It may be worthwhile discussing concerns with a health professional.

Fine motor control uses the small muscles. Examples of such activities are: coloring, painting, drawing, making crafts, doing puzzles, cutting, doing up and undoing zippers, buttons or snaps, opening and closing, fitting things together, taking them apart, piling things up, building with all different types of construction toys, picking up, holding on, pinching, turning things, using eating utensils or tools and, of course, printing. For many children, left or right hand preference is established.

Just before going further, there is a very important advisory note. Typically, fine motor skills develop later in boys than in girls. This is normal, expected and common. It is not unusual, abnormal or surprising. In addition, evaluating fine-motor skills is only assessing *development*, it is not assessing the *child*. Please keep these points in mind as you note a 1-for a skill your child is not yet able to do, 2-able to do at a beginning level, 3-able to do most of the time and 4-a skill at a well-developed level.

The first skill is building a tower of 6-10 blocks, before it falls over. Piling them up is easy for the first few and gets more exciting as the tower gets higher.

Puzzles vary in complexity and size and involve thinking skills, too, but as a ballpark, can your child complete a simple puzzle of 7 or more pieces?

Another fine-motor skill is being able to copy or draw two lines that cross, one up-and-down line and one side-to-side like a plus sign +, and a circle, o.

Drawing a person is also used as a way to assess social and emotional development, as well as fine-motor, as most children will be able to draw, at least, a head with some facial features. At this age, sometimes the arms and legs are only attached to the head not yet a body, but there should be 4 or more body parts in addition to the head.

By age five, children can copy some of the letters in their name and some can cut with scissors about a pinkie width on either side of the line.

For children just starting to use scissors, or needing more practice cutting, play-dough is great. It's easy to cut and doesn't have any lines to follow. It's just lots of fun to turn into tiny bits and pieces, smoosh it back together and cut again, especially for kinesthetic kids. Although it doesn't vacuum well off carpets, it will come off hard surfaces.

These above skills are representative of physical development in terms of gross and fine motor control.

Helping children develop their muscles and co-ordination can be done quickly and easily and here are a few ideas for them to practice or, for more fun, to do together:

Tired bird: Stand on one leg, hold the other up, close eyes and snore loudly for a few seconds. Switch legs. This helps develop body equilibrium (balance).

X's and O's: Cross left hand to right shoulder, then right hand to left shoulder several times; left hand to right hip, right hand to left hip several times; move down to knees. This is called crossing the mid-line and is important for brain development; remember the right side of the body communicates with the left side of the brain, and the left side of the body with the right side of the brain. These crossings of the mid-line (a line through the middle of the body from head to feet) are the X's. Finish off with some big self-hugs; these are the O's (or you can give some to each other).

Kids in Space: Move slowly through the house (maybe picking up things as you go) as if you were floating in space. Use big, slow arm and leg actions. Use a slow, spacey voice and provide a running commentary—oh, I am getting too close to the table, I will move my arm and then my leg. Now, I am far away from the door, etc. This encourages spatial orientation, that is the awareness of the body and the space around it in relation to people and objects. Having your child give the running commentary and listening to it gives you an idea of co-ordination and development and how s/he describes movement and space.

Robots: This game can be used to turn all kinds of work into fun. Dust the furniture like a robot or clean a room like one, all the time using a robot voice and dialogue. "Pass. Me. The. Towel. Hang. It. Up. Again." This develops body and movement awareness.

Walk Like a Duck: Or an elephant, or a dinosaur, or hop like a bunny, swim like a fish, perhaps, as you go to the car. Lots of muscle fun. My suggesting in desperation to a dawdling darling to gallop like a horse worked, once or twice.

Shadows: This game can work so well it is best to use it sparingly. Have your child follow you around and do exactly what you do!! Then switch and you do exactly what s/he does.

Stuck to The Chair: Pull a chair out so there is a little room around it and tell your child that s/he can sit on it, stand behind it, lay across it, whatever, as long as it is a safe position, but one part of the body, any part, must be stuck to it, an arm, leg, tummy, hip, etc. You may be lucky enough to get those extra 2 minutes when you need to finish something.

Action Songs: Who says the Hokey Pokey words have to be: "You put your right hand in?" "You put the dirty clothes, in the laundry hamper. You put the dishes on, the shelf in the cupboard." Make up whatever you need.

Simon Says: Adaptations to an old favorite. Simon says brush your teeth. Simon says pick up your socks. Simon says snuggle into bed. Let your kids be Simon, too, but be wary. "No, Simon did Not say I have to give you another bowl of ice cream and stand on my head. Ha, ha."

Fine motor skills can be promoted with making crafts, coloring, painting, play-dough, cutting things out of magazines, puzzles, folding, building with all kinds of construction toys and more. Some children find it more difficult to focus on small-muscle tasks as opposed to large muscle actions, so here are some suggestions to try.

Stuffie back-rubs: Have your child make a pile of stuffed toys. Close eyes and give one stuffie a back rub. Guess which one it is by the way it feels.

Dough shapes: Use a plastic knife to cut shapes out of pie or cookie dough. Bake them and once cool have your child close eyes and guess the shape. If it's the right guess, the prize is s/he gets to gobble up the cookie. If not, you get it. Hints are allowed, of course.

Monsters: Use some scraps of fabric, yarn, tags, or pasta and let your child glue them onto cereal boxes cut into monster shapes.

Ghosts: Old, white men's shirts are great for practice doing up lots of buttons to play ghosts.

Monster Salad: Choose a variety of small items, such as blocks or toys and a big unbreakable bowl. Using the salad tongs let your child pick up the little objects and make a salad for the monster (recruit a stuffie or a grown-up for the monster).

Cereal Roads: Put some dry cereal with little bits, like Cheerios, in a bowl. Let your child place these on a mat to make roads, curvy ones, straight ones, zigzags. The 'car' that 'drives' down the road is a spoon and your child is the crane that picks up the bits, drops them in the spoon and empties them into a tummy. Yum.

These kinds of activities not only enhance small muscle development but also encourage focussing on a small-scale activity. Concentration is like a muscle that needs practice too but the tasks can be challenging and fun at the same time.

Review: To review this section, five-year-olds have amazing energy. This seemingly endless supply of 'go' can be used to develop large muscle control and co-ordination. Focussing and concentration are like muscles that need to be strengthened and can be piggy-backed onto fine motor activities. Typically, fine motor skills develop later in boys than in girls. Again, our road reminders are:

How do I know if my child is ready for kindergarten?

What does my child need to learn before kindergarten?

How do I best get my child ready and provide ongoing support?

Differences between how boys and girls learn will be the topic in the section after next, as well as how to put all this evaluation information about readiness altogether.

Chapter Five
A = Academic Readiness (there is a reason for A not being first)

Academic Readiness Skills and Rating

This issue is the one that seems to worry parents the most. It urges them to ask: How much should my son or daughter know to be ready for kindergarten? What is required? Now, I can't answer for all states and provinces regarding requirements but I can give you some basic expectations for numbers, letters, counting, categorizing, patterning, auditory and visual memory, focussing, phonological awareness, etc, etc.

However, before I do, I need to let parents know, especially those who are sending their first one off to school, that *how* a child learns is part of this package, not just *what* a child already knows. Some of this is learning style: Does your child learn something when s/he watches and observes—a visual leaner? Do you need to explain everything a few times— an auditory learner? Has it been more effective to take his or her hand or body and practice over and over—a kinesthetic learner? Underneath it all is the skill of *knowing how to* learn.

How quickly does your child learn something new? Has it been slow and steady progress, or nothing, nothing, nothing…then, got it all of a sudden? Is your child able to remember things and build new skills from them? Yes, your child may be able to count up to 100, but is this just parroting because s/he has a super ear and memory or does your munchkin have an idea of what numbers are all about? Does your child understand the underlying pattern and how we can use this pattern?

There's ten items here, so, for this section, just mark numbers 1-4 right beside them. I'll do them in the same order as the checklist, (see intro section). You can continue using the 1-4 scale: 1-not yet, 2-sometimes, 3-most of the time and 4-all the time. And, I wish I could tell you that a whole column of 3s and 4s means definite readiness and this will translate to A grades on report cards but there's more to it. Two children could both score a 3, but have different levels of understanding. As we're doing these ten, I'll ask a few questions that you can think about.

My child can:

1. count 1-10: If your child has little interest in numbers that would be a 1 and indicate that some counting activities at home would be helpful. If your child can accurately count up to five that would be a 2, counting up to ten independently would be considered a 3, more than that a 4. What happens, though, if there is an interruption? Does you child have to start over again at one to get to ten or can s/he start at any number?

2. make groups of 1-5 things: That is, can accurately count out five blocks or five toy cars. Knows right away if you said it was okay to have three cookies but there's only two on the plate. Can tell if a group of four things is more than two. As before, if your child is starting to do this but it's not so accurate, that would be a 2, groups of five items a 3, groups of more than five would be a 4, not yet making and counting groups would be a 1. If you take one item away, does s/he notice and correct to one number lower or is it necessary to start counting again from 1 to find out how many?

3. complete patterns: If you go red sock, blue sock, red sock, — ?? s/he knows that the next sock is a blue one. That's figuring out what comes next or identifying. Can s/he correct a sequence? What happens if you ask your child to make a pattern? Assign a 1 for no idea of patterns, 2 if your child can finish a simple pattern but not yet create one, 3 if your child can make a pattern with two kinds of things, and 4 if your child can use more than two items or make more complex patterns.

4. sort into groups: These are toys with wheels and these are toys without wheels. Placing objects into the correct group is a basic skill. Supplying the label for the group and making one's own groups are more advanced skills.

5. tell same/different: These two spoons are just the same but this one is plastic, so its different. Sock and supper start the same. Sun and boot are different. Rate1-4.

6. sing a simple song: Old Macdonald or the Wheels on the Bus. How quickly does s/he pick up a new song? Again, jot down a 1,2,3, or 4.

7. listen to a short story without interrupting: Is this just looking at the person reading and being lost in space or is this following along with the story line and understanding it, being able to guess what might happen on the next page, supplying a plausible word using the context? 1 being not yet, 2 beginning, 3 involved in the story, 4 perhaps even recognizing familiar words or reading.

8. identify rhyming sounds: What rhymes with hat? fat, cat, rat, sat, mat. Which word sounds like sun--run or bed? This is more a yes or no, than 1-4.

9. draw a person figure: with at least a head and 4 more body parts. Use a 1 for not yet drawing, 2 for just a circle head, 3 for head and at least 4 body parts, and 4 for a head, arms, legs, feet, hands, features, etc.

10. either sing the letters in the alphabet song or recite a few of them. Can your child recognize some letters? My name starts with a J and so does Jumping Jenny. 1 would be little interest in letters, 2 some interest in letters though perhaps confusing with numbers, 3 can sing most of them and identify a few, and 4 has considerable familiarity with letters.

This list of 10 activities could certainly be longer but it gives parents an idea of some basics that most children will know. Because children develop at different rates, some children will not yet be interested in these school-type activities. But working on them at home, before school starts helps all children. When your child does learn a new skill, acknowledge this matter of factly. After all, learning new things is only to be expected. Children are quite capable. This is another example where we might inadvertently give a message contrary to our intention. We are thrilled and excited when our children (and students) learn a new task, but if we show that, children think they have done something out of the ordinary, something unexpected. Instead, since we do expect them to acquire new skills we sometimes need to treat this as everyday.

How to help children who are just not interested in academic-type work:

If your child isn't interested, what can you do? One suggestion is to piggy-back some of these activities onto things that are interesting. For instance, dinosaurs can be pretty motivating for counting, sorting, drawing, and patterning. To help practice cutting skills use play-dough. It's a lot more engaging than paper.

Start work-tasks with a couple of focussed minutes and gradually increase the time. And speaking of time, you don't need to squeeze your clocks to find it. Learning activities can be done right alongside all the other things that you already have to fit into your day. The section on communication and language suggests ideas that correspond to rooms in your house. This time, let's use the clock and go from breakfast to bedtime with ideas to support cognitive (mental) development.

Breakfast: "Good morning to you. And how many bowls of cereal does your tummy want to eat today? One bowl for one tummy sounds like it goes together. How many bowls would we need for two tummies? How many for three?" Pancakes are great for math, especially if they are small, because then one tummy could maybe eat 10 but make them much smaller!! This needs lots of counting and, for those ready for a challenge, it also introduces counting by tens. Making two eggs for each person introduces counting by twos. Count the dishes as you wash them or load them into the dishwasher. See if anybody at the table can name the letters on the cereal boxes. Compare how many people in your house prefer orange juice and how many like apple. And that was just breakfast.

Getting dressed: This is a great time to learn colors. And vocabulary and numbers. Sequencing, too. Do you put socks on first or shoes?

On the way out: Talk out the sequence, "First we go out the door, then we unlock the car. Oops, forgot to walk down the stairs." Sequencing is an important foundational skill for much learning at school. It's very challenging to describe a sequence backwards.

Going somewhere: On the way to the car or bus, count the steps. What happens if you take bigger steps; do you need more steps or fewer steps? Make a pattern, walk, walk, walk, hop, walk, walk, walk, hop, walk, walk, walk, runnnnn to the bus.

Bus trips: These are lots less boring and humdrum when there's something to watch for. How is one street different from the one before? How is it the same? What are the shapes on the street? Any letters or numbers? What groups of things?

Grocery stores and malls: These locations are learning-activity brain candy. Colors, sizes, shapes, letters, sounds. One day count all the circles you see, another time the squares, the rectangles, the triangles. What shape did you see most often? Was there one shape that was hardest to spot? Add in two descriptors at the same time, such as red + circles or blue + squares.

At the table time: So far, the suggestions mentioned do not require paper and pencil, nevertheless they are good readiness activities that will help your child build the focus and attention needed for independent work. When it comes to spending some time in the kitchen or at the table at daycare have some kid-friendly learning tools such as paper, pencils, crayons, and scissors for school-type work.

Does your child have a particular interest that you can build an activity around? Is there a holiday, birthday or family visit coming up that can be exploited for some craft-creating time? Any newly-found, exciting treasures? Sometimes the most ordinary objects can be the used. My daughter used two soda pop caps for eyes to make a picture of a face. A popsicle stick may become the mast for a sailboat picture, complete with cotton-fluff clouds and blue-wool ocean.

Drawing is not one of my natural or even acquired talents but I keep practicing. Dinosaurs are one of my favorite things to draw and are motivating even for children with little interest in crayons. Coloring a picture for someone special can entice a reluctant child to pick up a crayon.

Play-dough is inexpensive to make at home and can be used for reinforcing shapes, colors, numbers, letters, counting, spelling names and easy words, imagining, telling stories, sharing, fine muscle skills, and more. As mentioned earlier in this section, it is very motivating for developing cutting skills.

Chocolate pudding will function as a supreme motivator, if needed. Put a spoonful or two on a plate. With clean fingers, draw some letters of the alphabet. Or draw some basic shapes: circle, square, triangle and rectangle. You'll never hear complaints about having to practice printing a name with this ultimate trick. Licking is allowed between letters, as long as each person has a separate plate.

In the backyard: What a great time/place for science lessons. What's the weather like today? Was yesterday warmer or cooler? Notice the sky, the clouds, the trees. Talk about seasons and seasonal change. Parks are wonderful resources for all kinds of learning about the environment but even in the heart of the city there will be ants and bugs to notice and study. And, we always have weather. Children are natural weather forecasters. Windy, unsettled days seem to trigger unsettled behavior in kids. (Did anybody else's son come up with the idea of trying to pee the letters of his name? At least, it was outside.)

Eveningtime: Evenings can be low energy times and even five-year-olds can help prep and clean up after dinner. The kitchen sink is like a mini-science lab for 'discovering', using water and a few containers. Watch how the water pours. It takes the shape of any container. Which containers hold more water than others? How many spoons of water to fill up a cup?

Bathtime: Bath time allows for more and bigger containers. What floats, what sinks? Practice counting, are there more noses in the tub or are there more feet? How many towels are in the bathroom? Are there more white ducks or yellow ones? Are there 3 buttons on your pajamas or are there more?

And in many families, story time: Vary reading books with making up stories. Reading and enjoying books is the single most important activity. Statistics are mind-boggling. Children who have been read to at home develop enormous brainbank accounts of words that they understand and a huge audio track of stories. Even if you do not have much time to read, aim for 3 times a week.

In a study conducted of kindergartners, those who were read to at least three times a week as they entered kindergarten were almost twice as likely to score in the top 25 percent of literacy tests than children who were read to less than three times a week. National Institute for Literacy (2006), The Early Childhood Longitudinal Study.

Imagine being able to jump your child into the top quarter of the class, just by reading to him or her 3 times a week!

Any time of the day Voice and Touch: If your child has difficulty sitting still and focussing, here is something you could try. Sometimes using a low or soft voice forces a child to slow down and listen. Using touch can also be helpful. This is something, as a teacher that I can't do at school, but sitting on the floor behind a child to share a book and giving a shoulder rub or back scratch will help most children to slow down. Point out to your child that s/he is slowing down, breathing softer and slower. Again, gradually increase the time so as to get longer and longer periods of sitting calmly and quietly. If you can, vary the times of day. Being still is, actually, an *activity*. It demands muscle control and body awareness noticing where tension is held in the body. Being still is not just a question of relaxing.

At some point in time, observe how your child is tackling an activity so that you will have some information about his or her learning style. You may be better able to motivate your child to learn something new, if you have an idea of how s/he most prefers to learn.

Children, and adults, have different learning styles; some like to listen and learn through words. These are auditory learners. Others like to watch and learn through images. These are visual learners. Some like to touch and feel and learn through their bodies. These are kinesthetic learners, (play-dough is a super tool for them). Every one of us can use all these learning systems; it's a question of preference and of the learning task. No matter how each child learns best, it's important to vary activities to encourage development of all learning styles.

Summary: To summarize pre-academic readiness: *children develop at different rates and stages and have different learning styles*. In any case, there are some basic concepts that most children at this age have learned or are currently learning. These include: rote counting to 10, making groups of 1-5 objects, patterning, sorting, distinguishing same and different and recognizing a few letters. Most can sing a simple song, listen to a story and draw a person with a few body parts. Being able to rhyme shows a basic

---

phonological awareness, that is an understanding of and using parts of words. There are lots of simple, ordinary activities that families can do at home to provide support for academic readiness.

And why is academic awareness last? Readiness is so much more than knowing abc's and 123's. Unfortunately, academics seem to get most, if not all, of the attention. By leaving it to the last, the importance of the other aspects of readiness have not been so over-shadowed.

Do you now have some answers for these three questions?

How do I know if my child is ready for kindergarten?

What does my child need to learn before kindergarten?

How do I best get my child ready and provide ongoing support?

And that's it for an in-depth look at readiness.

Chapter Six
Overview of Basic Readiness and Development

"While we try to teach our children all about life, our children teach us what life is all about." Anonymous

Using the checklist and your notes, you now have a much more complete picture to answer the first question: **HOW DO I KNOW IF MY CHILD IS READY FOR KINDERGARTEN?**

For the second question, **WHAT DOES MY CHILD NEED TO LEARN BEFORE KINDERGARTEN?** there is a summary at the end of each developmental area to give general guidelines. This varies, to some extent, according to regions and cut-off dates. In some places, kindergarten is optional. Attendance at school is not mandatory until grade one.

Throughout the book, I've suggested easy and quick activities that help you answer the third question: **HOW DO I GET MY CHILD READY AND PROVIDE ONGOING SUPPORT?**

Children develop at different rates, and boys and girls may even develop in different sequences. Your readiness evaluation may be an entire page of 3s and 4s but it is very common to have a mix of 1,2,3, and 4. This shows some strong areas, some that need extra support. Does a whole page of 1 mean Not Ready? Yes, no, and maybe. And I'm not waffling or sitting on the fence or avoiding answering the question. It *can* mean that, or it can be reflecting a lack of experience and stimulation. It *does* indicate a need to ask some more questions and investigate possible causes. On the other side of the road, for those children that seem more than ready with a page of 3s and 4s, issues come up during the year that raise questions, too.

Parents are children's first teachers and homes are children's first classrooms. Many readiness and learning activities can be combined with what families are already doing using resources that are already available. When children do enter school, Parent Involvement is a key factor in educational success.

Kindergarten readiness is not just academics. Social and emotional skills need to be included, as well as self-help, language and physical development.

Please remember each child is a unique individual. Children develop at their own rate, at their own pace, in their own way. They each have their own interests and talents as well as challenges and concerns. For all children, these early years before school even begins, are tremendously important for learning.

No matter your child's date of birth, or the region where you live, there are more ideas for readiness in the next section. Plus, I've reviewed some new research so we can fit in how readiness differs for boys as opposed to girls.

Part Two
Other Concerns

Kindergarten this year... Kindergarten next year...

Chapter Seven
Close to the Cut-off and/or Children Who Don't Seem Ready

Kindergarten attendance is not mandatory in all states and provinces. Nor, is there a standard cut-off date for birthdays as to when a child can enter kindergarten. While most areas have a date in September, it can vary all the way from having to be five by June 1 before starting kindergarten to being able to *start* at four as long as the child turns 5 before March 1 of the next calendar year. The entry cut-off dates can vary within a state or province as well with the dates being a local option. In some areas, kindergarten is an all-day program and in some only a half-day. One year I taught in a rural school and kindergarten was only two days a week because of bussing. Two very long days for little ones.

Deciding what to do can be really tough if your child's birthdate falls in an optional part of the year. Because many parents have asked this question over the years, I can offer some more points to consider. Usually, the more pieces you have to a puzzle the easier it is to see the whole picture.

Birthdate: Not all children with early birthdays are comfortable attending kindergarten and not all children with late birthdays have a real struggle at school. So much depends on the child, and the family.

Readiness: Tools, like the developmental checklist I gave you, can provide more information or information in a concise format. Does your child seem to have some developmental lags or delays? Does your child seem to have a general level of readiness?

Moves: Is the area where you are living currently just a temporary arrangement? Are you anticipating a move in the next year or two to a state or province with a very different cut-off date? This will affect your child's social group and is another factor in your decision. Are you planning to take a year off to travel or live in another country?

Family dynamics: Do you have two children close in age? Will they be attending school in the same year, just because of the school cut-off dates? Would you prefer a gap of one year or two years between them? What works best for your family in terms of transportation, work, daycares, blended family siblings or other issues?

Graduation end: This is really gazing into the crystal ball but is another piece to the puzzle. Will your child be going off to college or university at the age of 17 or 18? Is there a chance post-secondary education will be near home, so you can offer that extra degree of keeping an eye on the situation? Or far, far away—and you won't be close enough to offer support and guidance?

Peer group: It's kind of nice if your son or daughter and friends get their driver's license, start to date, and join sports teams with age limits at about the same time. Peer groups form at school and late birthdays may mean your child has to wait. Wouldn't life be easier if school and community groups got together and sorted it out? Sometimes there's an advantage to having your child drive and date a year later, in terms of age, than the other kids, as is the case when kindergarten start is delayed.

Growth Spurt: It's not fun being the youngest in the class and the smallest. In some families the children, particularly the boys, have early growth spurts, while in others the shooting up doesn't happen until the last few months of high school. It's not easy towering above classmates either, whether you are the oldest or the youngest, male or female.

Child's Reactions: What kinds of body messages are you picking up from your child? The decision-making power will rest with the parents but what are your child's reactions when you talk about or visit the school?

What would happen during the wait year? This may be the biggest aspect to consider. Yes, your child will be one year older. Will this be another year at home? At preschool or daycare? What kind of readiness support will your child receive during this wait year? What kind of readiness support does your child need? Your child may need some time to gain independence and adjust socially so another year with some support at peer play-groups would offer that. Perhaps, there is a lag in pre-academic skills and spending the upcoming year and the following year in kindergarten would be an alternative.

In some regions, children can attend kindergarten for two years. Some parents start a child in kindergarten, closely monitor the situation during the first few days and weeks and then make the decision to wait a year.

Knowing what other parents have done may help. I've provided some real, not hypothetical, experiences. (The names have been changed.)

Emily had a late November birthday. Her big sister was only one year older and Emily liked to do everything her big sister did and often did it with her. They were practically the same size and Emily was confident and assured. She went off to kindergarten at the age of four and had a great year.

Jason had a late November birthday, too. His concentration and focussing skills were beginning to develop. He had little interest in being a member of a group. He went off to kindergarten but he did not have a happy, carefree year. The teachers met with his parents the very first month about waiting a year but he remained in kindergarten and went on to grade one. In grades one and two, despite having extra support at school, he struggled with learning to read. He graduated from secondary with average marks but decided to wait a couple years before going on to college *because he didn't feel ready.*

Ahmed's birthday was also late in the year. At the age of four, he really enjoyed the playing part of school but after the whole kindergarten year he only knew a few numbers and still could not accurately make groups of 1-10 objects. He had learned to write his name but fine-motor skills were a challenge and, compared to his peers, he was small and not very well coordinated. He went off to grade one with his friends, and with some extra assistance from the student support team, had a fine year. Despite the challenges, Ahmed was keen and he worked hard. His parents spoke little English but helped at home by being interested in his work. Looking back, Ahmed probably had little experience and stimulation at home and this contributed to the developmental lags. His determination and extra effort contributed to his catching up.

Kevin had an April birthday. There was no question he was eligible to start kindergarten in September, as he was *already* five. His parents had separated, he had recently moved and for the first time he had attended daycare. Though he had an amazing vocabulary and extraordinary background knowledge in science, he showed little interest in paper and pencil activities. He still couldn't print his name nor draw anything beyond scribbles. He seemed troubled and worried. *Two* kindergarten years with the same teacher, the same dayhome, and later counseling, gave him stability and a chance to develop socially. In his last year of high school, he grew like the proverbial weed and was no longer the second smallest in class, even though he was the oldest. After graduation, he went on to a post-secondary institute and became a radar and communication technician.

Sara had a birthday in December. A wee bit of a thing, she chattered happily and started kindergarten but was easily distracted. Concentrating, basic early skills, playing with others all seemed to lag. Before the end of the first month, I asked her parents to come in and recommended that Sara begin kindergarten the following year. She stayed in kindergarten and at the end of the year, the school team suggested having another round of kindergarten before grade 1. Sara had made progress over the year but we felt she would really benefit from another year to build on it. In grade one, despite support at home and at school, she struggled with reading and math. She began to be discouraged and even quieter. Although Sara continues to grow and learn each year, she struggles and at the end of grade three, when she again met with the school team, her mother remarked that she wished that she had started Sara a year later.

These are a few children that have been in my kindergarten classes. As you can see, they are all different and the issue of readiness impacted girls as well as boys. The kindergarten-this-year-or-next is such a difficult decision because we are not just dealing with the present but are trying to predict the future.

Being objective about our children is quite a challenge. Advice is varied and confusing and profuse (especially on the internet)! Each child is unique and there are as many angles to consider as a dodecahedron. Two important questions are:

IN WHAT WAY(S) DOES MY CHILD NOT SEEM READY FOR KINDERGARTEN?

WHAT KIND OF READINESS SUPPORT WILL FILL AN INTERVENING YEAR?

Truly, I've been there and done that with this very same decision and discussed it with other parents. Remember your own learning channel preference. If you are primarily auditory, talk it out. If you are visual, draw it out. If you are kinesthetic, try your decision on for size and see if it fits. Or do all three.

It is sometimes possible to start kindergarten, to monitor the situation closely those first few weeks and, then, to review, and change, your decision. Some areas may allow two years in kindergarten.

Chapter Eight
Children With Learning Challenges and/or Exceptional Learning

ADD, ADHD, ADDH, APD, ASD, DCD, FAS, LD, LLD, NVLD, OCD, PDD, SLD, SI, SpLD. Looks like a strange code but these are all abbreviations for various learning challenges in children—and there's more! This doesn't include the asia's and the xia's. (No, there won't be a test on these at the end.)

Sometimes, learning challenges have already been diagnosed for some children. Readiness for these children is more complicated. Parents and caregivers need to communicate with the school as early as possible. Some kindergarten programs will have in-take evaluations with a school-based team. It is helpful to have as much information as possible with you when attending these meetings. Take along medical reports, pediatric recommendations, outlines of intervention to date, developmental assessments, and anything else which you feel is pertinent. A plan for the child can be developed to put into place as many resources as possible to support the child's readiness for and success at kindergarten. Supporting children with learning challenges requires frequent communication, creativity, and home-school-community teamwork.

Kindergarten teachers may detect other children with different learning needs. Sometimes, further assessment and evaluation is recommended by the classroom teacher as learning challenges surface. The earlier that intervention and support occurs, the better for the child. As with the child already identified, the more resources that can be gathered the better it will be for the students *and* the parents, teachers and caregivers.

All children have special gifts and talents but "gifted" children have exceptionally advanced learning in comparison with most children of the same age. Bright and gifted refer to different levels. Bright children are interested, attentive, and learn easily. At school, they work hard, know the answers, quickly understand and grasp new ideas, have good memories, and seem to absorb information. Gifted children are curious, seem to spread out their attention and already know. At school they do not need to work hard; they ask questions, have complex ideas, and expand on information given to them.

A "gifted" child may have extraordinary skills in one area but not others. A child with noteworthy abilities in math or music may have social skills that are average or not yet developmentally appropriate. Kindergarten may be too easy and too hard at the same time. Communicating with the school and teacher about your child is likely the best course of action.

All children have different strengths and areas that require more practice and development. At each age and level there is an extensive range. It is important to balance the needs of the child and to look at the whole picture of readiness so that your child has the best chance for success.

Chapter Nine
Is Readiness Considerably Different for Boys and Girls?

Is there a difference in readiness depending on gender? Is readiness the same for both girls and boys? The easy answer is yes, there are some differences and yes, there's some sameness. But since that's not at all helpful, I'll skip those questions and go on to highlight *how* readiness can be different for boys as compared to girls.

Boy brains and girl brains process language differently. To quote Dr. Sax, the author of the book Boys Adrift: "The language area in the brain of a typical 5-year-old boy...looks very much like the language area in the brain of a 3½-year-old girl." (Boys Adrift: An ULTRA-short summary.) No wonder that language and communication skills tend to be more advanced in girls than in boys. Much information at school is presented verbally so doing some fun activities at home in this area will help support your sons.

Research has also noted another significant difference in terms of social and emotional development. "The female brain is predominantly hard-wired for empathy. The male brain is predominantly hard-wired for understanding and building systems." (Simon Baron-Cohen, *The Essential Difference: Men, Women and the Extreme Male Brain*) Boys and girls will understandably not express their emotions and feelings in the same way. They will not react to events the same way, either. This will also be reflected in their choice of toys and how they play. Although this is somewhat over simplified, boy-play will have lots of action and construction; girl-play will have lots of interaction. This same component is evident in boys' drawings. Boys tend to draw action while girls draw relationships and color things, (see later page).

Not only are there differences in the way male and female brains are hard-wired and in how they process information, there are differences in the senses, too. Much of this information comes from Abigail Norfleet James' book, *Teaching the Male Brain*. With regards to hearing, girls hear softer sounds better and boys have a higher tolerance for noise. (We needed research to tell us this? Our daughter used something as small as a shoelace for dressing up. Spoons were given sound effects by our son. I suspect many, many parents and caregivers, throughout the ages, have noticed this.) While girls may have sharper hearing, boys have the advantage in vision. Spatial skills too are stronger for males than females.

Boys also have a greater tolerance for pain and for cold. When we first moved to the coast after one too many prairie winters, I remember telling my son that as of the first of December, kids had to wear long pants to school. There may be other differences in skin sensitivity, as well. The senses of smell and taste are usually more accurate and sensitive in females.

With regards to readiness, girls are more ready to read, write and calculate than boys. There is *tremendous* variation in individuals, so it is not fair to only use stereotypes but our expectations and activities need to be adapted when we respond to boys and girls with lots of figuring-out tasks for boys and talking time for girls. This is not news for parents. Why didn't scientists just ask?

Boy Drawing:
A balloon exploding...

Girl Drawing:
This is for you...

Chapter 10
PLAY-the Essential Component of Healthy Learning!

The Crucial Component—PLAY

Play is so essential to the healthy development of children that it has been enshrined by the United Nations High Commission on Human Rights in its Convention on the Rights of the Child. Why is play so significant? Quite simply, because play is how a child learns. The activity does not matter; it could be building with blocks, cuddling a stuffie, putting together a puzzle or throwing stones in a puddle. It could even be washing the dishes or putting away the groceries. If a child is eager and having fun, creating, discovering and manipulating, this is play.

Children's programs and at-home activities need to include time for play. Through play, children connect their inner and outer worlds, increasing their knowledge and understanding and gaining confidence in themselves. Play enhances all aspects of development: social and emotional, physical, language and intellectual or cognitive. At school, play is built into the kindergarten experience and used as the vehicle for learning. At home, play-time is crucial.

Skills Developed Through Play Activities

The previous pages have started with skill development followed by suggested ideas. This part will flip the order and show what kinds of skills can be learned in a few activities. These are not just 'academic' or school-work skills.

Skills children learn:

Blocks and construction: lifting, pushing, pulling, weighing, carrying, balancing, manipulating, stacking, fine and gross motor co-ordination, visualizing, shapes, counting, spatial orientation, co-operating, imagining and pretending.

Puzzles: problem-solving, fine motor skills, sequencing, patterning, comparing, visualizing, part-to-whole relationships, goal setting (finish the puzzle), perseverance, achievement, responsible use and care of materials.

Water: (at home, this can be a sink or tub) observing, pouring, estimating, experimenting with concepts of volume, visualizing, comparing, concentrating, relaxing, personal care, learning the names of body parts. Playing with water has been shown to be very calming for children.

Play-dough: hand-eye co-ordination, building small muscle strength, visualizing, vocabulary, language, sensory information such as texture, shapes, letters, numbers, problem-solving, planning. Play-dough is wonderful for cutting practice.

Drawing and Crafts: how to use tools such as pencils, crayons, scissors, glue, and other materials, creating, appreciating, exploring color, shape, line, size, and dimension; representing, organizing, taking risks.

Make-believe: imagining, creating, language, sharing, speaking and listening, exploring different roles and emotions, negotiating, caring, nurturing, planning, using toys in meaningful ways, awareness and relating to others, self-knowledge.

Stories and books: listening, making pictures in the mind, language, imagining, vocabulary bank, questioning, predicting, connecting experience to new knowledge, forming letter-sound association, associating text with meaning, auditory memory and discrimination, visual memory and discrimination.

Cooking: measuring, following instructions, making meaning from pictures or text, small muscle development, vocabulary, sequencing, science concepts such as heat changes chemistry, reversible/non-reversible physical changes, whole/parts.

Music: auditory memory and discrimination, listening, sound vocabulary, comparing, contrasting, predicting, matching, patterns, brain connections, math. Information from research has shown that music and math are related and that they use some of the same brain pathways and connections. Music has spaces between notes, and notes have ascending and descending order. Math has spaces between numbers and numbers have ascending and descending order.

Nature activities: (walking around the block, going to the playground or park, visiting a farm or zoo, etc) discovering, developing curiosity, appreciating similarities and differences, respect for wild-life, caring for the environment, needs of others, life cycles, seasonal changes.

These are only some of the competencies that a child can learn through play. Nevertheless, these few activities do show how much children learn when they are playing. Adult support not only includes how much we do with our children but *how much we let them do by themselves*. It is up to us to make sure their day has time so they can just play. As a parent or caregiver, no matter how little or much energy or time you can spend with your children one of the most important things you can do is to *ensure and safe-guard their essential play-time*.

We do not quit playing because we grow old.
We grow old because we quit playing.
George Bernard Shaw

Part Three
More Than ABC and 123

*Educating the mind without educating the heart
is no education at all. Aristotle*

Chapter of Questions
Beyond the Checklist

The checklist and the corresponding chapters in this book are based on *what* a child needs to learn before kindergarten. Much research is based on this. Government and community programs for children focus on ABC and 123 developmental content and skills. Beyond that, children's success in kindergarten is also influenced by *how*. And this is far harder to put into a list framework. It's even hard to define.

As a parent, raising my own two children, I worked on *what* the kids were learning. We counted and read and sang songs and played letter games. Now, as a grandmother, I've been able to expand the experience and really watch *how* a child learns. For instance, my granddaughter wanted to close the buckle on the highchair straps. At first, she had difficulty sliding the two ends together. She pushed away adult help and tried over and over. I thought about options; she could have become frustrated and cried for help, grown tired and found something else, or kept at it. What determines what a child does? Is it personality or is it learned? Or both? In any case, I started thinking about these *hows*.

An obvious one is: *how* does your child feel about learning something new? Some children are delighted when they face a new learning task. Some are dismayed and anxious. Dr. Martin Seligman, in his book Learned Optimism (1980) writes that children have already developed optimistic or pessimistic perceptions by the third grade. I am not a renowned and respected psychologist so I can only speak from experience, but for some children their outlook is noticeable much earlier. Support would mean helping a child feel confident and comfortable about learning and viewing the world. Another *how* is how your child reacts when the task is hard. Frustration is a common experience for all of us. How does your child handle frustration? We can help children by acknowledging their feelings and giving them some tools. At school, I sometimes give an upset child a piece of scrap paper to scribble over. Or we list off some silly words—oh, pizza, oh macaroni, oh, cookies—until the child giggles and then, we try again.

Resilience can be added to the *hows*. Where does the ability or skill to get 'back in the saddle' come from? Some children are never phased by failure; some are devastated. Is this character or practice? And patience? Why do some children find it such a challenge to wait? Is impatience just concentrated enthusiasm? Are there additional and significant *hows*?

Sometimes, it is not the learning activity that is the challenge but *how* your child learns. Research on learning styles, multiple intelligences and *how* the brain functions is providing teachers, parents and caregivers with more information so that we can better meet children's learning needs.

Readiness and success are also shaped by values. Acceptance, gratitude, competitiveness, and the importance placed on family and education are factors, too. How do we support learning important values? What are the most significant ones? You get the point. A discussion along these lines is beyond the scope of this book but it is a worthy one for families. It certainly raises questions. In comparison, questions about when children should start school and how much they should know and be able to do are much easier to answer!

These are the things I learned:
- Share everything.
- Play fair.
- Don't hit people.
- Put things back where you found them.
- Clean up your own mess.
- Don't take things that aren't yours.
- Say you're sorry when you hurt somebody.
- Wash your hands before you eat.
- Flush.
- Warm cookies and cold milk are good for you.
- Live a balanced life - learn some and think some and draw and paint and sing and dance and play and work every day some.
- Take a nap every afternoon.
- When you go out in the world, watch out for traffic, hold hands and stick together.
- Be aware of wonder. Remember the little seed in the Styrofoam cup: the roots go down and the plant goes up and nobody really knows how or why, but we are all like that.
- Goldfish and hamsters and white mice and even the little seed in the Styrofoam cup - they all die. So do we.
- And then remember the Dick-and-Jane books and the first word you learned - the biggest word of all - LOOK.

The kindergarten children are confident in spirit, infinite in resources, and eager to learn. Everything is still possible.

Robert Fulghum (author of All I Really Need to Know I Learned in Kindergarten)

Conclusion
Kindergarten Success

Success depends upon previous preparation,
and without such preparation there is sure to be failure.
Confucius

While I disagree with Confucius, that failure is the sure outcome of lack of preparation, I can attest that preparation certainly makes whatever we are doing easier. The 'whatever' in this case, is preparing our children for kindergarten. And we can start the preparation right now, no matter the age of the child. *When we start small, we start smart.* As I quoted in the beginning:

Children who are ready for school from the day they start kindergarten have a better chance to do well in each grade and finish high school. *(Human Early Learning Partnership-HELP-at UBC, January 2010)*

For a child, going off to kindergarten is much the same as an adult going on a trip to a new country. The difference is, instead of a suitcase, it's a backpack. When we travel, we prepare. We make a list and pack our bags. In this book, I've included a list for readiness and packed in tons of ideas, suggestions, and activities to prepare you and your child for the school journey that starts even before kindergarten. With this, you are well prepared.

Preparation promotes readiness and readiness contributes to success. (Barbara Allisen, you can quote me ☺.)

To zum up the entire book, (no, that's not a typo; I meant to use the z as a sort of play on the letters of a-z), I believe that the children who have turned over rocks, watched the paths that the raindrops leave on a window, and have sung silly songs with their parents and caregivers are prepared. They have developed a foundation. This foundation is the expectation and experience that adults have wonderful lessons to share with them and everything else builds on it. These children are ready to learn.

We reveal the world of adventures with the language in stories and books, explore the mystery of numbers, and unlock trunks with treasures of science and discovery, when we play and learn with our children. We hold the special keys to a magical kingdom that we can open up to our children by building on those playful and teachable moments that are part of every day. What a gift for us to use and to give to our children!

May the time you spend getting ready for kindergarten and the kindergarten year, itself, be filled with the wonder of discovery, the fun of creating and the joy of play.

Little moments can make big memories.

Extracurricular

To book Barbara Allisen for any of these extracurricular activities please contact:
Toll free: 1-866-796-2272 or
check the website: www.123kindergarten.com

Speaking Topics:
Parents and caregivers have lists of questions regarding kindergarten readiness.

With over thirty years of classroom experience, Barbara Allisen can give answers as to how to best prepare children for school and beyond. Practical, parent and child friendly, Barbara shows how to find minutes hidden in busy days to help children get ready for learning. Home is Grade Start for children's education.

Preschool educators, daycare operators and childcare workers are often the transition between home and school. Communication between centers and schools is not always possible. Barbara can provide a view from inside the classroom to help facilitate the change from childcare facilities to the school system and maximize children's potential for success.

Workshops: Ready, Set, Kindergarten
Offer your future students and parents a get-ready-for-kindergarten orientation mini-conference. Barbara helps your group organize and present 90 minutes of preparation for school activities. The Ready, Set, Kindergarten program has a registration desk for families, welcome address, and five 15 minute, break-out mini-sessions. These hands-on sessions include how to read stories to promote literacy,

using play-dough for readiness skills, fun exercises, songs and games, basic readiness with crafts, and early math concepts using everyday materials. Session facilitators come from within your group who best know your families and children.

***This workshop can be part of a fund-raising program for your facility.

Two Stars and a Wish:
Combine an evening presentation to your group with a next day mini-conference for families. And the wish? 1 2 3 Kindergarten books for families to take home.

***This can be included as part of the fund-raising package for your facility.

Consulting:
One-on-one time with Barbara Allisen to discuss your concerns about your child. Friends and family offer advice based on their experience, but it may not match yours. Barbara can offer her professional perspective to help you with your decisions.

Eat, Play, Kindergarten Monthly Membership:
Each month, kids get seven activities to do at home that help them learn basic readiness skills. Projects at their level, (younger children need more parental help, older ones need less). Children sing, explore, draw, read-along, make and taste, exercise and count as they play, learn and get ready for kindergarten.

Made in the USA
Charleston, SC
07 November 2013